SIMP
TAI CHI

HINKLER
BOOKS

D0517569

Editor: Margaret Barca
Creative Director: Sam Grimmer
Photography: Peter Wakeman
Design: Katherine Power

First published in 2003
by Hinkler Books Pty Ltd
17-23 Redwood Drive
Dingley Victoria 3172 Australia
www.hinklerbooks.com

Printed and bound in China

ISBN 1 7412 1499 8

CONTENTS

INTRODUCTION

Tai Chi is an ancient form of meditative exercise which originated in China, and is easily recognised by its slow, captivating movements. Originally Tai Chi was developed as a martial art but it is now practised by millions of people around the world to improve and maintain good health.

Tai Chi represents a way of life, helping people to meet day-to-day challenges with energy whilst remaining calm and relaxed inside.

The History Of Tai Chi

The origins of Tai Chi have been disputed for many years. According to Chinese history, Tai Chi began in the Chen Village in the Henan Province of China. This area also includes the Shaolin Temple, famous for its Kung Fu. Tai Chi follows the principles of Yin and Yang, the two opposing forces of life, such as night and day, positive and negative, open and closed. These principles are incorporated into Tai Chi as hard and soft movements. The initial stages of learning involve the slow and soft movements of the Tai Chi Form. More advanced learning combines hard, fast power with soft, flowing strength to produce a supreme fighting art.

In more recent times, several Tai Chi styles have developed, the most popular of which is the Yang style, named after the Yang family.

The Simplified Tai Chi Form

The Tai Chi Form taught in this book is a simplified routine, which still contains the traditional characteristics and postures. Unlike most traditional forms, however, this routine requires only a small amount of space and can be easily practised in your own home. Should you wish to expand your knowledge of Tai Chi, this book will form a solid basis for more advanced learning.

THE BENEFITS

The delight of Tai Chi is that anyone can practise it, any time, anywhere and in almost any state of health. There is no age limit.

The many reasons for practising Tai Chi include to:
- improve health
- reduce stress levels
- increase your energy
- improve concentration
- have a better quality of sleep
- strengthen bones, muscles and joints
- increase flexibility
- improve digestion due to internal massage
- improve heart and lung function
- prevent age-related ill health
- be a moving meditation to quieten and focus the mind
- use as self-defence.

Tai Chi's slow movements provide the opportunity to relax and strengthen your body, without risk of strain or injury. It is also particularly suitable for the elderly, as it improves balance and strength, preventing injury from falls. Many people begin Tai Chi with injuries or ill health and their primary focus is to aid their recovery.

The first noticeable benefit is usually a feeling of relaxation and wellbeing. Becoming aware of which parts of your body are tense, and how to relax them, results in a calmer mind and body. The benefits of Tai Chi quickly flow into other areas of your life, allowing for a more relaxed and healthy approach to daily activities. After a period of time you should begin to sense your own energy or Chi.

Regular practice is the key to progress and with repetition the movements will become automatic, allowing your Tai Chi to be relaxed and flowing.

PRACTICAL MATTERS

As with any new exercise regime, if you have any doubts about your health, consult your health professional before beginning. Start your Tai Chi slowly and gently, gradually building up the number of repetitions. Always listen to your body and stay within your own capabilities. Proceed at your own pace to avoid strain or injury.

You need no special equipment for Tai Chi. Loose clothing is best. You can do the movements in bare feet or wear comfortable shoes or socks.

You will need a room with an open area of approximately 2 square metres. Tai Chi can be done anywhere, even outside. Doing Tai Chi outside surrounded by nature adds a whole new dimension and stimulates the senses in many ways.

The morning is the best time to do Tai Chi, as it relaxes your mind and gives you energy for the day. But any time of day will be beneficial. You can practise when you come home from work to wind down, or at night to promote a deep restful sleep. There is a wide selection of Tai Chi music available, which can provide soothing background music.

TAI CHI BASICS

CHI

The Chinese believe we all have an internal energy called Chi, which exists within our body. It is stored in the lower abdomen in an area known as the 'Tan Tien' and runs through channels called meridians. Chi gives us our vitality and allows us to grow and develop. When we are first born we have an abundance of Chi but by the time we reach old age it is declining. With the regular practice of Tai Chi, we are able to replenish some of this energy.

Interruptions to the flow of Chi can cause ill health. One of the many benefits of Tai Chi is that it enhances the flow of Chi throughout the body and discourages blockages.

Correct posture during Tai Chi is essential for the flow of Chi and to avoid unnecessary strain.

POSTURE

The basic posture principles of Tai Chi include the following:

• Your whole body should be relaxed but not limp.

• Your head should be held high. Imagine it is suspended from above by a piece of string – this lengthens and straightens your spine. Your chin should be pulled in slightly.

• Your shoulders and chest should be relaxed, not hunched or tense. Do not force your shoulders back.

• Your pelvis should be slightly tilted forward with your bottom tucked under, which straightens the lower back.

• You should always aim to be standing straight, not leaning forward or back. Pay particular attention to this when doing forward pushing movements.

• As a general rule, one foot should not be moved without first shifting your weight to the other foot.

BREATHING

Breathing is an essential component of the Tai Chi Form. Your breath should be slow and deep, breathing down to your abdomen rather than high and shallow in your chest. With this method of breathing, your abdomen should rise and fall rather than your chest. Breathing deeply is relaxing and beneficial for the body. It also provides more oxygen, which allows for greater stamina.

Generally, the in-breath should be related to open movements and the out-breath corresponds to pushing or closing movements. Breathing in this way helps develop Chi and internal power.

OPENING STANCE

The Opening Stance is a relaxed posture used at the beginning of many of the exercises.

1 Stand with your feet shoulder-width apart. Your weight should be evenly distributed over both feet and your knees slightly bent. Your feet should be pointing straight ahead.

2 Tilt your pelvis forward slightly so that your bottom is tucked in and your lower back is flattened.

3 Completely relax your shoulders and allow your arms to hang loosely by your sides.

4 Face forwards and make sure your head is held upright as if suspended by an imaginary string from above. Pull your chin slightly back so that your neck is straightened.

BOW STANCE

Bow Stance (or Bow and Arrow Stance) is a fundamental posture of Tai Chi. It is a stable and grounded stance and other postures use the leg positioning of Bow Stance.

1 Begin in the Opening Stance Posture

2 Move your left leg directly forward about 30 cm. Make sure you keep the shoulder-width distance between your feet when you step forward.

3 Move your weight forward until your knee is bent and directly over your left toes.

4 Your right leg should be straight (but the knee is not locked), with your toes pointing slightly away from your body. Turn your hips to face the same direction as your right toes, but face forwards.

This is the Left Bow Stance. The Right Bow Stance is with the right foot forward instead of the left.

EMPTY STEP

The Empty Step is a posture where all of your weight is on one leg. The other leg is just touching the ground but bears no weight. This step is used throughout the Tai Chi Form, either as a means of transferring weight from one stance to another or as a posture.

TAI CHI HAND

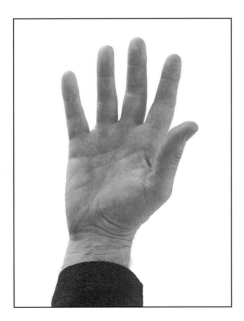

The hands play an important role in Tai Chi. They are the focal point of your vision and project your Chi outwards. During Tai Chi, your eyes generally follow the leading hand.

Your hands should be opened but in a relaxed manner. Don't allow tension in your hands as this blocks the flow of Chi. Your fingers should be nearly straight but with a slight curve. You may feel the presence of Chi in your hand as a sensation of warmth.

WARM-UP

Purpose *Warm-up exercises are not only to prepare the body for the Tai Chi Form – they are also highly beneficial in their own right.*

These exercises are designed to loosen all the major joints and warm-up the associated muscles, tendons and ligaments, to prevent any strain or injury. When you begin the warm-up exercises, start slowly with 3 or 4 repetitions and gradually build up to 7 over time. If you experience any pain or discomfort, stop that exercise or scale down the number of repetitions. Always listen to your body. The exercises should be done smoothly and in a slow, relaxed manner, allowing your body to be free from tension.

Don't be alarmed if you hear a few noises from your joints when you first start exercising. Your joints are being exercised in a wider range of movement than they are used to and any noise or discomfort should diminish with practice. However, if you feel any pain or have any concerns, consult your health professional.

For the maximum health benefit, aim to do these exercises daily.

NECK EXERCISES

Benefits *These exercises increase flexibility, strengthen the neck and also relieve neck tension.*

UP AND DOWN

1 Begin in the Opening Stance posture. Relax your shoulders. Allow your head to slowly roll forward until your chin rests close to your chest.

2 Next lift your head and allow it to gently move backwards until you are looking upwards. Only move your neck as far as comfort allows, then return your head to facing forwards again. Repeat slowly.

3 Start with 3 complete movements, building up to 7 over time.

Neck Exercises
(continued)

SIDE TO SIDE

1 Begin in the Opening Stance posture and then slowly turn your head to the left. The aim is to end up looking over and behind your left shoulder but initially just turn your head as far as you feel comfortable. Then smoothly bring your head back to the centre and around to the right shoulder.

2 Bringing your head back to the centre again is one full movement. Repeat in a gentle motion.

3 Start with 3 repetitions and increase to 7 over time.

HALF CIRCLE

1 Begin in the Opening Stance posture and turn your head to the left.

2 Allow your head to drop down slowly until your chin is near the centre of your chest. Carry on this movement and raise your head up to the right, looking out over the right shoulder.

3 Then drop your head again and repeat the movement in the reverse direction.

4 When you are looking out to the left again, this is one full movement. Start with 3 repetitions and build up to 7.

NOTE

Only ever do half circles with the neck. Never move the head in a full circular movement which bends the neck backwards whilst turning.

SHOULDER EXERCISE

Benefits *The shoulder area is one of the most common places to carry tension. This movement frees up and relaxes the shoulders. It is of particular benefit for arthritis sufferers.*

1 Begin in the Opening Stance posture.

2 Place your fingertips on your shoulders. While keeping your fingertips on your shoulders, rotate your elbows in a circular movement, making the circle as large as possible.

3 Do 4 circles forward and then 4 backward, working up to 7.

HIP EXERCISE

Benefits *This exercise strengthens the pelvic and leg muscles, loosens the hip joint and promotes good balance.*

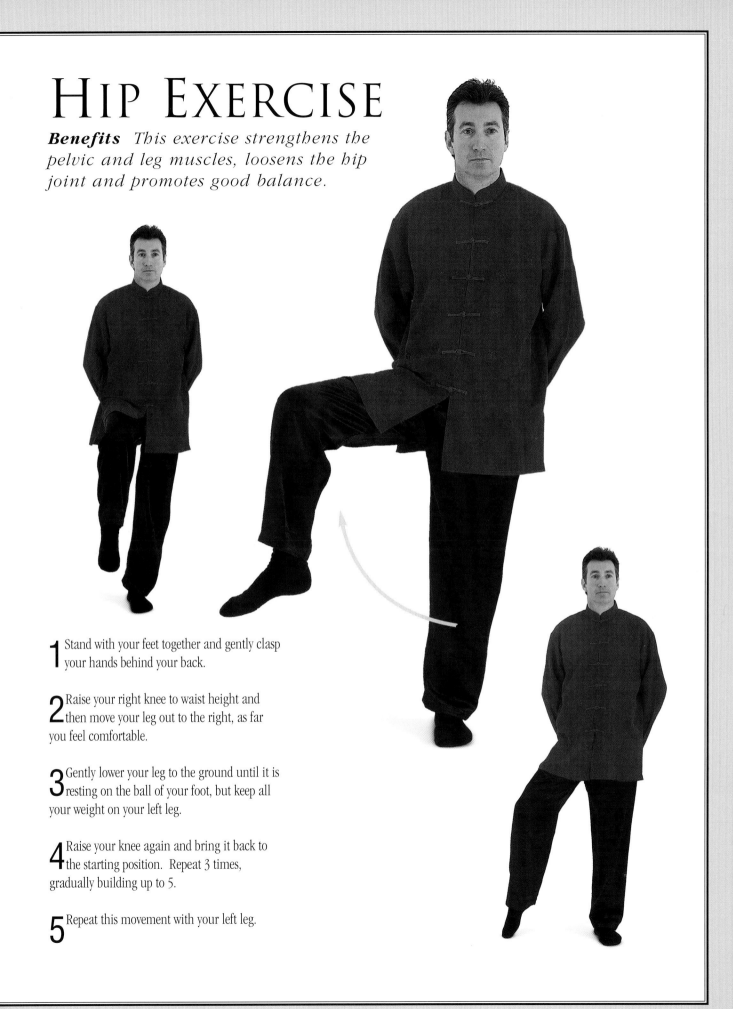

1 Stand with your feet together and gently clasp your hands behind your back.

2 Raise your right knee to waist height and then move your leg out to the right, as far you feel comfortable.

3 Gently lower your leg to the ground until it is resting on the ball of your foot, but keep all your weight on your left leg.

4 Raise your knee again and bring it back to the starting position. Repeat 3 times, gradually building up to 5.

5 Repeat this movement with your left leg.

WAIST EXERCISE

Benefits *This exercise strengthens the lower abdominal and back muscles and promotes flexibility in the hip joints. It also relaxes the lower spine.*

1 Begin in the Opening Stance posture. Place your hands lightly on your hips.

2 Whilst keeping your shoulders relaxed and your head still, rotate your waist to the left in a wide circular movement.

3 Do 4 rotations to the left and 4 to the right, gradually increasing to 7 over time.

KNEE EXERCISE

Benefits *This movement strengthens and tones the muscles and ligaments around the knee joint.*

1 Stand with your feet together and your knees slightly bent.

2 Place your hands on your knees and rotate your knees to the left in a circular motion. Do 4 rotations to the left and 4 to the right, building up to 7 over time.

3 As your strength and flexibility increases, gradually try to bend your knees lower.

ANKLE EXERCISE

Benefits *This exercise promotes flexibility in the ankles.*

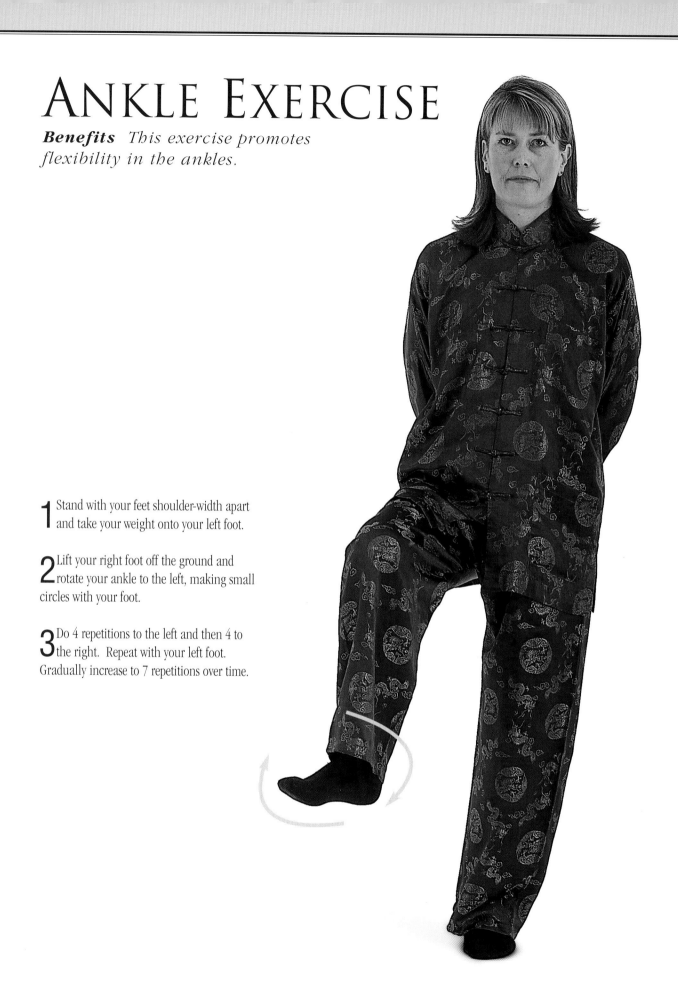

1 Stand with your feet shoulder-width apart and take your weight onto your left foot.

2 Lift your right foot off the ground and rotate your ankle to the left, making small circles with your foot.

3 Do 4 repetitions to the left and then 4 to the right. Repeat with your left foot. Gradually increase to 7 repetitions over time.

SHOULDER RELAXATION

1 Stand in the Opening Stance posture and keeping your arms down, raise your shoulders up as high as you can lift them. Hold for two seconds and then release, allowing your shoulders to drop back down into their relaxed position.

2 Repeat once or twice.

NOTE

This movement releases tension in the shoulder area and can be done at the beginning of any exercise or before the Tai Chi Form. It is also a good quick exercise to carry out whenever you become aware of tension in your shoulder or neck area.

OPENING FORM SQUAT

Benefits *This exercise strengthens the legs, knees and the lower back.*

1 Begin in the Opening Stance posture.

2 Breathe in and raise your arms to shoulder height, with your palms facing downwards.

3 As you breathe out, bend your knees and allow your arms to drop slowly at the same time. Make sure you keep your back straight.

4 When you have gone down as far as you comfortably can, turn your palms to face upwards. Breathe in and stand up slowly.

5 When your arms reach shoulder height, turn your palms over and repeat. Build up to 8 squats over time.

NOTE

Try to co-ordinate the lowering of your arms with the sinking of your body and your out-breath.

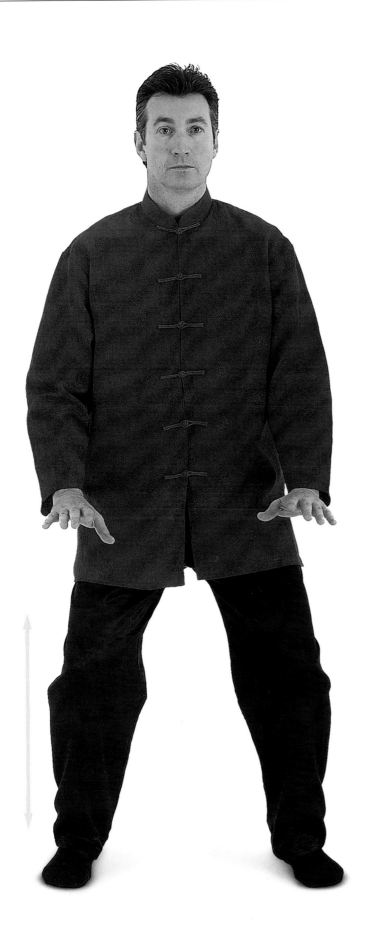

SWINGING ARMS

Benefits *This exercise relaxes the whole body, in particular releasing tension in the shoulders and the upper back area. It also keeps the spine supple.*

1 Begin in the Opening Stance posture.

2 Turn your waist to the right. At the same time, pivot your right heel, with your toes up.

3 Do not consciously move your arms but allow them to swing naturally with your body movement.

4 Now turn your waist to the left and pivot on your feet again, this time raising your left toes.

5 Make your movement flowing from one side to another with no pauses. As you increase your speed, your arms will naturally swing outwards and wrap around your body.

Carry on this movement as long as you wish – it's very relaxing.

NOTE

Make sure you keep your
shoulders and arms
completely relaxed and let
your waist drive the
movement.

HEAVEN & EARTH

Benefits *This is a very relaxing movement, which helps cleanse the lungs of stale air and invigorates the body with fresh oxygen. It is good for relaxing and strengthening the lower back. With practice it lengthens the hamstring muscles, increasing flexibility. Heaven & Earth also calms the mind.*

1 Begin in the Opening Stance posture.

2 As you breathe in, raise your hands together in front of your chest, your fingers pointing upwards.

3 Extend your hands upward to their full extent, looking up at your hands.

4 Turn your palms out and turn your head to look at your left hand. Your eyes should follow your left hand throughout the first movement.

5 As you breathe out, open your arms up in a large circular movement. As your hands reach shoulder height, bend your waist, keeping your back straight.

6 Continue to let your hands drop right down in front of you, leaning forward as far as you can comfortably reach.

7 Turn your palms to face forward, breathe in and raise your arms up, keeping them straight. Slowly straighten your back.

8 When your arms reach shoulder height, bring your hands in towards your body and push your elbows up.

9 Breathing out, allow your palms to push down to waist height. This is one full movement.

10 With each movement, alternate which side you turn your head to. Build up to 6 or 8 repetitions.

PARTING THE CLOUDS

Benefits *This movement increases leg strength and stamina, and promotes flexibility in the shoulder joints. As this exercise is based on the Tai Chi Form, with practice you will begin to develop your Chi and you may sense it as warmth between your hands as you push forward.*

1 Begin in the Opening Stance posture.

2 Step directly forward about 30 cm with your left leg. Make sure you keep the shoulder-width distance between your feet when you step forward.

3 Bring your hands together at waist height, palms facing each other but slightly apart, fingers facing forward.

4 Breathing out, move your weight forward and push forward with your hands.

5 When your arms have almost reached their full extension, the hands open up and your palms turn to face downwards and slightly outwards.

6 Breathe in and as you pull back, shift your weight to your right leg. At the same time, your hands come back in a wide circle and return to their starting position.

7 Do 4 of these exercises with the left foot forward and 4 with the right foot. Work up to 7 repetitions over time.

NOTE

As you repeat this exercise, keep your movements in time with your breathing. Breathe out as you push forward and in as you pull back. Be careful when pushing forward not to let yourself lean forward. Try to keep your back straight and your shoulders relaxed.

PUSHING CHI

Benefits *This movement enhances co-ordination, improves concentration and encourages relaxed breathing. It also promotes the development of Chi.*

1 Begin in the Opening Stance posture.

2 Extend your left arm out in a half-circle, with your hand at chest height. Your palm faces the centre of your body and your fingers point to the right.

3 Put your right hand close to your body, just higher than your left hand, with your palm facing away from you and your fingers pointing upwards. Allow your right elbow to relax down.

4 As you slowly push forward with your right hand, pull in with your left. The hands move at the same speed and pass each other.

5 When the right arm is almost fully extended, the left hand should be in close to your chest. Then turn the right hand over so that your palm faces you and your fingers point to the left, dropping to chest height. At the same time, your left hand raises up higher than your right hand. Rotate your hand so that your palm faces away from you. Allow your left elbow to relax down.

6 Now your left hand pushes slowly forward while your right hand pulls in to your chest.

7 When your left arm is almost fully extended, rotate your hands again so that you are back to the starting position. This counts as one full repetition. Build up to 7 repetitions over time.

NOTE

When you have mastered the hand movements, practise breathing out as your right hand pushes forward and breathe in as it pulls towards you.

WAIST ROTATION

Benefits *This meditative movement improves co-ordination and relaxes the mind and the breathing. It also promotes flexibility in the spine and the waist area.*

1 Begin in the Opening Stance posture.

2 Extend your left arm out in a half-circle, with your hand just below chest height and your palm facing downwards.

3 Move your right arm up by your right side, with your fingers pointing upwards and your palm facing to the left. Raise your palm up to temple height.

4 As you slowly move your waist to the left, your arms move with your body.

NOTE

The waist drives the movement in this
exercise. The arms just follow. Remember to
keep your shoulders relaxed. Once you have
mastered this exercise, breathe out as you turn
to the left and in as you turn to the right.

5 When you have reached as far as you can
comfortably turn, drop your right hand down to lie
in front of you, palm facing downward. At the same
time, drop your left hand down and back in a circular
motion. As you raise the left arm back up again, turn
your hand over so that your fingers point upward and
your palm faces to the right.

6 Turn your waist back to the centre and then across to
the right.

7 When you have reached as far as you can
comfortably turn, drop your left arm down and
sweep your right hand out until both hands come back
to their starting position. Returning to the centre
completes one full repetition. Build up to 7.

THE FORM

You are now warmed up and ready to begin Tai Chi. Watch the Form on the video a couple of times first, to give yourself an overview. Use the video in conjunction with the book to help you understand the steps and further illustrate the postures.

Remember the following important Tai Chi principles:
- all the moves are done slowly and smoothly
- your head should be up straight and your chin tucked in slightly
- your shoulders and chest should be relaxed
- your pelvis should be slightly tilted forward
- you should always aim to be standing straight, not leaning forward or back
- as a general rule one foot should not be moved without first shifting your weight to the other foot.

Note that each movement follows on from the next. At the end of the Opening Movement you are ready to start Part the Wild Horse's Mane. The position you are in at the end of Part the Wild Horse's Mane is the starting position for the next movement.

Now, let's start!

OPENING MOVEMENT

1 Stand with your feet together, hands relaxed at your sides, palms facing your thighs.

2 Shift your weight onto your right foot and move your left foot a shoulder-width apart.

3 Turn your hands so your palms face backwards and as you breathe in, raise your arms to shoulder height.

4 Breathing out, bend your knees and allow your elbows and arms to drop until your hands are at waist height.

OPENING MOVEMENT
(continued)

5 Shift your weight to your left foot and turn your body to the right, pivoting on your right heel.

6 At the same time, raise your right hand up as your left hand drops down until it is underneath your right hand, palms facing each other.

7 Transfer your weight to your right foot and bring your left foot next to your right. Keep all your weight on your right foot.

8 This the Right Hold Ball Position.

PART THE WILD HORSE'S MANE

1 Step out with your left foot towards the front.

2 Whilst turning your waist, raise your left arm up in a curved movement to shoulder height, palm facing you. Drop your right arm to waist height, palm facing downwards, fingers facing forwards.

3 Transfer your weight onto your left leg and straighten your back leg.

NOTE

Your feet form the Bow Stance Posture. Your right leg should be straight but don't 'lock' your knee.

WARD OFF

1 Step up, placing your right foot next to your left. Move your right hand forward and under your left hand, into the Left Hold Ball Position.

2 Step out with your right foot to the right.

3 Shift your weight onto your right leg and straighten your left leg into the Bow Stance Posture.

4 At the same time drop your left hand to waist height and raise your right arm in a curve until your palm is at chest height, wrist opposite your centre.

This is the Ward Off Position.

GRASP THE BIRD'S TAIL

1 As you turn your waist to the right, extend your arms out to the right, with your left palm facing upwards and your right palm facing downwards.

2 Sit back, bringing your weight onto your left leg. At the same time pull your hands down to your left hip.

3 Turn your right hand and raise it up to just below your chest height, while your left hand turns to face your right hand, palms touching.

4 Press forward with your hands, shifting your weight onto your right leg

GRASP THE BIRD'S TAIL
(continued)

5 When your arms have almost reached their full extension, flatten your hands, your left hand moving over your right.

6 Open your arms to shoulder width, sit back and take your weight onto your left foot, raising your right foot onto its heel.

7 Your hands pull back and down to your waist in an arc, with palms facing away from you.

8 Transfer your weight forward again and push forward with your hands.

SINGLE WHIP

1 Bring your weight back onto your left foot, turning your waist and right foot around to face the front. At the same time, let your right arm drop down until your hand is in front of your body.

2 Move your left hand in a circular movement out to the left, then back to the centre again, while raising your right hand until your palm faces you.

3 Transfer your weight back to your right foot and move your left foot next to it.

4 Move your right hand straight out in front of you and turn your palm facing down with your fingers pressed together to touch your thumb. At the same time, move your left hand up to your right forearm, with your palm facing you.

5 Step out to the left with your left foot. As you turn your waist, move your left arm around until it is in line with your left foot and rotate your hand so that you are looking at your index finger.

6 Move your weight forward so your legs form the Left Bow Stance posture.

This is the Single Whip Position.

STRUM THE LUTE

1 Transfer your weight onto your right foot and turn your left palm downwards.

2 Turn your waist and left foot around to face the front.

3 Then take your weight back onto your left foot, while flattening your right hand.

4 Pick up your right foot and place it on its heel.

5 At the same time, rotate your hands until your thumbs are facing upwards and move your left hand to half-way along your right forearm.

WHITE CRANE SPREADS ITS WINGS

1 Turn your palms downwards.

2 Pull down with both hands towards your left hip, as you turn your waist and right foot to the left.

3 Raise your left hand to shoulder height and curl your right hand under to form the Left Hold Ball Position.

4 Sit back, moving all of your weight onto your right foot and bring your right hand up and out to the right, to head height. Rest your left hand near your right forearm.

5 Your left foot moves forward and out to the left in an Empty Step. All your weight remains on your right foot. At the same time move your arms apart, until your right hand comes to rest directly opposite your right temple and your left hand is down by your left hip, fingers facing forwards.

This is the White Crane Position.

BRUSH KNEE

1 Turn your waist to the left until your right hand faces you.

2 As you turn your waist back, drop your right hand down to the right in an arc, with your palm facing upwards. Move your left hand over the top until it comes to rest at your right elbow, palm facing downwards.

3 Bring your left foot back close to your right foot.

4 Step out straight ahead with your left foot.

5 As you transfer your weight forward, move your left hand down and around until it comes to rest by your left knee, fingers facing forward. At the same time, bring your right hand in towards your head and then push it out directly in front of you.

This is the Brush Knee Position.

CLOSING FORM

1 Transfer your weight to your right foot and curl your left toes around to face the front.

2 Turn your waist and your right foot to the right, pivoting on your heel.

3 At the same time, move your right arm around in a circular motion and move your left arm out to the left, up to the same height, both palms facing away from you. Look to the right.

4 Bring your weight back to your left foot, curl your right toes to face the front.

5 Move your right foot to a shoulder-width distance from your left and drop your arms until they cross in front of your body.

6 Stand up, raising your hands to shoulder height.

CLOSING FORM
(continued)

7 Rotate your hands until your palms are facing downward.

8 Open your arms to a shoulder-width apart and move them down to your sides.

9 Bring your left foot back to rest next to your right foot.

CONCLUSION

WELL DONE!

There is an ancient Chinese proverb which states that even the longest journey starts with the first step. You have taken your first step towards learning Tai Chi.

Tai Chi can be a life-long study, with the benefits and rewards relative to the amount of time and effort you put into it. With regular practice your Tai Chi will become more relaxed, reducing your stress and tension levels. This will enable you to gain the full benefit of this graceful art.

The *Simply Tai Chi* book gives you a basic introduction to Tai Chi. Should you wish to expand your knowledge, there are many experienced instructors, who can further your training. Tai Chi is a vast subject with different forms and variations, so you will need to find a style and instructor that suit you.

People begin Tai Chi for many different reasons, be it stress reduction, physical fitness or spiritual awareness. Whatever your reason, we hope your journey is a fruitful one.

ABOUT THE AUTHORS

GRAHAM BRYANT first learnt Tai Chi in England in the 1980s. In London Graham studied with Professor Li, head of Physical Education at the University of Beijing, who taught very traditional and precise Tai Chi. Graham is proficient in many forms and styles of Tai Chi and has taught it for many years. In 1998 Graham travelled to the Chen Village in the Henan Province of China to visit the birthplace of this ancient form of exercise. Graham is currently studying the martial aspects of Tai Chi.

LORRAINE JAMES first studied Tai Chi in Melbourne in the 1980s. Since then she has furthered her Tai Chi, learning both Yang and Chen Style forms. Lorraine has taught Tai Chi and especially enjoys seeing the freedom of movement older people achieve after practising Tai Chi. Lorraine is a certified Classical Homoeopath and practises on the Gold Coast, Australia.